McDonnell Douglas Harrier II AV-8B B Plus

Luis Díaz-Bedia Astor

MCDONNELL DOUGLAS
CORPORATION

Schiffer Military History
Atglen, PA

On the front cover: A stationary AV-8B Plus moments before landing on board the *Príncipe de Asturías* aircraft carrier. On the sides it has two external fuel tanks and an air-to-surface AGM-65 Maverick missile. *(Luis Díaz-Bedia)*

Dedication

Dedicated to Raúl, Ramón y Ángel

Acknowledgments

The author wishes to thank Lieutenant Commander Jorge Flethes Serrano, Commander (Eng.) José Navarro Rodero, Ship lieutenants Angel Sáiz Padilla, Manuel Rodríguez Giner, Francisco Guerrero Flores (Eng.), Warrant Officer Luis Cabeza Barrios, Vicente Rodríguez Sosa and especially Lieutenant Ricardo Huertas Díaz and Corporal (V) Jesús Vivas García for their valuable contributions.

Translation from the Spanish by Linda Robins da Silva.

The original Spanish edition appeared in 2011 under the title:
McDonnell Douglas Harrier II AV-8B/B Plus
by Reserva Anticipada, Inc., Barcelona, Spain.

Printed in China
ISBN: 978-0-7643-4264-6

We are interested in hearing from authors with book ideas on related topics.

Published by Schiffer Publishing, Ltd.
4880 Lower Valley Road
Atglen, PA 19310
Phone: (610) 593-1777
FAX: (610) 593-2002
E-mail: Info@schifferbooks.com.
Visit our web site at: **www.schifferbooks.com**
Please write for a free catalog.
This book may be purchased from the publisher.
Try your bookstore first.

In Europe, Schiffer books are distributed by:
Bushwood Books
6 Marksbury Avenue
Kew Gardens
Surrey TW9 4JF, England
Phone: 44 (0) 20 8392-8585
FAX: 44 (0) 20 8392-9876
E-mail: Info@bushwoodbooks.co.uk.
Visit our website at: www.bushwoodbooks.co.uk

The prototypes for the Harrier II, known as YAV-8B, were in fact modified AV-8A aircraft, equipped with a metal replica of the new carbon fiber wing, with a more powerful engine which had more efficient air inlets and with new LIDs. *(McDonnell Douglas)*

The development of the AV-8B Harrier II

The two companies which made the first version of the Harrier AV-8, the British company Hawker Siddeley Aircraft and the U.S. company McDonnell Douglas began to consider, at the beginning of the 1970s, replacing this aircraft with another with superior features. The new machine, given the name AV-16, would have a wing with a larger surface with a revolutionary aerodynamic edge, and would be equipped with a more powerful engine than the AV-8, giving it a greatly increased load capacity and radius of action. However the program failed due to the anticipated high cost of the new engine and due to the fact that the requirements of the U.S. Navy and Marines on the one hand, and of the RAF and the British Navy on the other, differed to such a extent that it was problematic to reconcile them in the same model. The two companies therefore decided to follow independent paths towards developing a V/STOL (Vertical and Short Take Off and Landing) aircraft, called AV-8B by the Americans and GR5 by the British.

Compared to the AV-8A/C and GR3 aircraft, the two new projects would provide a plane with a larger wing surface, an elevated cockpit and longer fuselage. The fundamental difference between them was found in the construction of the wing. Whilst the British envisaged a metal wing, which could be used in the possible remanufacturing of the GR3 aircrafts, the Americans developed one in carbon fiber that incorporated a *supercritical* edge based on NASA research. In addition, McDonnell Douglas had also planned to use carbon fiber in the fuselage and empennage.

The lack of financial support by the British government for Hawker Siddeley/British Aerospace and the rights that it granted to McDonnell Douglas in regards to the percentage of participation in the construction of the new aircraft, meant that the British company eventually opted for participating in the technically superior, North American program. As well as the new wing, the AV-8B incorporated flaps of a new design and more modern LIDs (*Lift Improvement Devices*), situated in the ventral part of the fuselage to improve the lift on a stationary flight. The engine was a high power Pegasus engine, with more efficient air intake, made by Rolls Royce but with a 25% participation from Pratt & Whitney in the case of the American aircraft.

Due to the wishes of the U.S. Marines to undertake the aerodynamic tests with a life-size model, McDonnell Douglas used an AV-8A aircraft

A United States Marine Corps AV-8B aircraft at the Rota naval base. Although the aircraft belonged to one of the Harrier squadrons at Cherry Point, it was assigned to the HMM-162 – combined helicopter and Harrier aircraft unit – during its take off from a helicopter carrier.
(*Luis Díaz-Bedia Astor*)

to which was added a replica of the wing in metal, as well as the new engine with its air intake nozzles and LIDs. The results were satisfactory and it was decided to convert another two AV-8As to the YAV-8B version in order to carry out the airborne tests, due to start on the 9th of November 1978. These showed considerable improvements in the performance of the V/STOL system and in aircraft control. Due to the fact that the rate of aerodynamic friction was higher than expected, structural modifications were undertaken to reduce it. To improve the maneuverability extensions were added to the leading edge of the wings, at the height of the join with the fuselage, known as LERX (leading edge root extension). The new aircraft was slower than the AV-8A, but its flying characteristics, radius of action and load capacity were notably superior.

A Harrier GR7 of the Fighter Squadron No.1 of the RAF at the Rota naval base in the middle of September 1997. The protuberance of the NAVFLIR can be seen on the nose, as well as the in-flight refueling probe, and the *Intake suction doors* needed for the intake of additional air required by the engine during a stationary flight and the expulsion of gases from the RCS *Reaction control system*, which allows the plane to be controlled on slow and stationary flights which can be seen on the far left side. Some of the differing characteristics from North American built aircraft can also be seen, such as the aerials from the electrical interference equipment, situated on the underside of the nose, or the additional weapons station for the Sidewinder, under which is the chaff and flare launcher. (Luis Díaz-Bedia Astor)

AV-8B for the US Marine Corps.

In 1979 the construction of the first four AV-8B aircraft was approved, with the stationary flight tests commencing on November 5, 1981. Following them was a pilot series of twelve aircraft – the first undertaking its maiden flight on August 29, 1993 – and a limited series of twenty-one airplanes. Mass production began in November 1983 and although the aim was to produce 328 aircraft for the U.S. Marine, 286 were built in total.

The AV-8B was quite a different aircraft from the YAV-8B used in its development. The empennage and most of the rear fuselage were made from carbon fiber. The cockpit was raised, allowing the pilot a better view and leaving additional space underneath for avionics equipment. It was equipped with a zero-zero capability UPC/Stencel 10B ejector seat, able to eject from a grounded stationary position. The ARBS (Angle-Rate Bombing System) with video and laser tracking was installed in the nose. The cockpit contained a HUD SU-128 (Head Up Display) and a multifunction screen capable of showing information from the sensors related to take offs and landings, navigation, TACAN, loads and the condition of the engine. Some systems from the F-18 were installed, such as the HOTAS (Hands on Throttle and Stick), the AYK-14 mission

▶ The initial core of the Ninth Squadron at the production facilities of the McDonnell Douglas Company in Saint Louis. *(FLOAN)*

▼ One of the first three AV-8B delivered to the Spanish Navy, undertaking an in-flight refueling whilst crossing the Atlantic towards the Rota naval base, en route from Saint Louis, on October 6, 1987. *(FLOAN)*

computer, the ASN-130 inertial navigation system and the AN/AYQ-13 weapons control and management system.

The electronic warfare equipment was also from the Hornet: the AN/ALR-67 radar warning system, the ALE-39 chaff and flare dispenser and the two pieces of counter-measure equipment, although these, due to the reduced space available in the Harrier, were installed in an ALQ-164 pod. For communications two broadband UHF/VHF ARC-182 radios were chosen. For the pilot to input data into the computer a UFC (Up Front Control) was included under the HUD. The first aircraft used an F402-RR-404 engine which already incorporated

the new design of the front nozzles, designed to improve the efficiency of the air flow and increase the wing lift at low speeds. However, the engine for the mass-produced aircraft was the F402-RR-406, which incorporated a DECS digital control system to improve its efficiency.

To increase the offensive potential the Harrier II was given a 25mm General Electric GAU-12 Gatling-type cannon, with a container for 300 projectiles and a rate of fire of sixty projectiles per second. The cannon and the ammunition container are found in the two pods installed in the left and right ventral areas respectively, replacing the LIDs.

The first squadron of the Marines to take delivery of the aircraft was the VMAT-2-3, in charge of instructing new pilots. El AV-8B also replaced the AV-8C in the VMA-231, VMA-542 and VMA-513 squadrons, and the A-4M Skyhawk in the VMA-331, VMA-223, VMA-211, VMA-214 and VMA-311 squadrons. The VMA-331 was the first of the combat squadrons to take delivery of it, being declared totally operational in August 1985.

Harrier II for the RAF

In August 1981 the British and U.S. governments signed an agreement for the acquisition of the first sixty Harrier II aircraft for the RAF, intended to

Personnel from the Ninth Squadron and the *Flotille 59s* of the French Navy between an AV-8B and a Super Etendard at the Hyeres Airbase, at the end of an Exchange between both units, June 10, 1993. *(collection of Luis Díaz-Bedia Astor)*

During the *ALFEX 02/99* exercise, flight personnel from the Ninth Squadron install protective covers for various AV-8B equipment after an on-board landing. *(Luis Díaz-Bedia Astor)*

Ninth Squadron

Official patch of the Ninth Squadron with the *Harrier* with the number 9 in its claws. *Over sea and over land* – as the motto says in Latin – and *day and night* – which is more accurate since the inclusion of the Plus aircraft.

An AV-8B moving backwards to park – the nozzles are pointing forwards – after its landing aboard the *Príncipe de Asturias* during the *Tramontana 94* exercise. The practice of moving backwards was abandoned some time ago as the expulsion of gases to the front can result in the engine ingesting particles from the deck and because it overheats directional devices in the nose gear.
(Luis Díaz-Bedia Astor)

Initial patch offered by McDonnell Douglas when the Ninth Squadron was created, used on the shoulder by its pilots during the Unit's first years of activity

A stationary AV-8B on the port side of the *Príncipe de Asturias*, before crossing the deck for take-off, during the *ALFEX 01/96* exercise. (*Luis Díaz-Bedia Astor*)

equip the GR3 squadrons based in Germany. In turn, McDonnell Douglas and British Aerospace, BAE, signed another agreement leading to a greater role for the company in the production of the British airplanes and making it responsible for its final assembly.

The first flight of a British aircraft took place on April 30, 1985. Of the RAF airplanes, forty-one were built as GR5 variants, whilst the other nineteen were GR5A variants, incorporating modifications to allow them to later be converted to the GR7 Night Attack model.

The GR5 differed from the AV-8B: it had a Pegasus Mk105 engine and a Martin-Baker Mk12H ejector seat, part of the fuselage was reinforced, the GAU-12 cannon was replaced by an Aden revolver cannon of the same caliber, and weapons stations to upload in each band were added, dedicated to the Sidewinder missile. The electronic warfare system chosen was the GEC-Marconi Zeus, which includes a warning system and counter-measures radar, Plessey missile approach warning system and Bofors chaff dispensers in the Sidewinder missile stations. In terms of the avionics, the radios and the IFF were

The author undertaking a turn on board an AV-8B during a training flight in the summer of 1993. *(collection of Luis Díaz-Bedia Astor)*

replaced with other British manufactured models and a screen was added to show a digital map by the GEC Ferranti Company.

On May 29, 1987 the first GR5 aircraft was delivered to the RAF at Wittering airbase, although the start of pilot training was delayed due to some problems with the inertial navigation system, and again four months later when the planes were grounded whilst there was an investigation into an accident which cost Captain Taylor Scott, a BAE test pilot, his life, due to a problem with the design of the ejector seat. Finally on March 30, 1988, No.20 Squadron RAF (Operational Conversion Unit) in Wittering began flights, and in November of the same year No.1 Squadron RAF began to take delivery of the new aircraft, followed by No.3 in December.

The two-seat Harrier II

Initially the U.S. Marine Corps considered continuing to use the TAV-8A for the instruction of new AV-8B pilots. However the flight characteristics were so different that it was necessary to develop the TAV-8B, which only had two weapons stations installed as it did not have a combat mission. Of the twenty-five aircraft built, twenty-two were delivered to the VMAT-203 Squadron, which began to take delivery of them in July 1987, two were acquired by the Italian Navy, and one was used by McDonnell Douglas to carry out flight systems tests.

The RAF also decided on the acquisition of two-seat aircraft, but equipped like the GR7 version, with all its weapons stations and night combat capacity. This version was called the T10 and undertook its first flight in 1994. Most of these aircraft were incorporated into No.20 Squadron.

The AV-8B in the Spanish Navy

The Spanish Navy had had significant experience in the operational use of the Harrier AV-8A from its entrance into service in 1976. With a new aircraft carrier in construction, it wanted to modernize the fixed wing component of its Air Arm, so at the beginning of the 1980s it started a program for the acquisition of the Harrier II. On March 16, 1983 the purchase of twelve AV-8B aircraft was approved by the Cabinet and two years later by the Initial Core of the Ninth Aircraft Squadron at the Rota naval base. All its personnel undergo the relevant adaptation courses at the McDonnell Douglas facilities in St. Louis. In addition, the pilots from the Eighth Squadron receive their

Personnel from the Ninth Squadron preparing the armaments of an AV-8B in the parking area of the Rota naval base, during an Arming of the Fleet in April 1996. *(Luis Díaz-Bedia Astor)*

initial training on this model at the Marine air base in Cherry Point, North Carolina.

In September 1987 the Ninth Aircraft Squadron was formed, under the command of Captain Joaquín Arcusa Pinilla. On 6th October of that year the first three EAV-8B aircraft arrived in Rota the name includes E for España (Spain), from St. Louis, with North American pilots undertaking the longest non-stop flight of a Harrier II up to that date, covering a distance of 3,959 sea miles, lasting nine hours and five minutes, and needing eight refuels whilst airborne. On December 2 the next three aircraft arrived. The training flights followed and on the 14th of that month the Ninth Squadron carried out its first bombing exercise in the Gulf of Cadiz. On March 7, 1988 four aircraft carried out the plane's first night flight and on the 22nd of that month the first in-flight refueling by Spanish pilots was completed, with an Air Force C-130. On April 21 the Harrier II aircraft took part for the first time in a Fleet exercise, carrying out a strike on the Aeronaval Group.

Cobra
Patch with the emblem of the Ninth Squadron which came into use at the end of the 1990s.

The author with flying equipment in front of an AV-8B in June 1996. The equipment for Harrier pilots consists of fire-resistant flight coveralls, anti-G suit – which inflates when subject to accelerations, reducing the blood flow to the lower parts of the body; torso-harness – where the fixing points of the ejector seat are located; survival vest – on top of the previous equipment, with integrated float and holding various pieces of survival equipment; helmet with earphones, oxygen mask with integrated microphone, steel-toe capped boots to protect the toes during ejection and fire-resistant gloves. *(collection of Luis Díaz-Bedia Astor)*

Patch with the *Cobra* emblem of the Ninth Squadron, used from the middle of the 1990s and in this case belonging to a pilot with more than 500 hours.

Second lieutenant Angel Marco Hernández going towards his aircraft prior to a flight, in the parking area at the Rota naval base, in September 1997. (*Luis Díaz-Bedia Astor*)

On the April 28, 1988 the EAV-8B simulator, built by the Spanish company CESELSA, was officially handed over to the Spanish Navy at the Rota naval base. This considerably boosted the training of the pilots, allowing for the standardization of procedures and frequent practice of flights in active conditions, responding to emergencies and of different missions, including operations on aircraft carriers, land attacks and air interception, with the possibility of using air-to-surface and air-to-air weapons.

On May 15 the first detachment of the Manises airbase took place for bombing on the Caudé firing range, where the 25mm cannon was used for the first time. On May 17 three other aircraft were delivered to Rota, and on August 31 the tenth arrived followed by the arrival of the final two on September 15. On the 20th and 21st of the same month the pilots of the Ninth Squadron qualified on board the veteran *Dédalo*, and on the 20th and 25th they formed the first detachment from the Zaragoza airbase to bomb on the Bardenas Reales firing range. On October 3 part of the Squadron boarded the *Dédalo*, with five aircraft. On September 28 the AV-8B undertook its first landings on the *Príncipe de Asturias* aircraft carrier, which was in its first year of guarantee after being delivered to the Spanish Navy on May 30, 1988. For a number of months the aircraft participated in the operational qualifying of the modern Spanish aircraft carrier.

During the following years the AV-8B were used, together with the AV-8A until it was decided to transfer them to the Thai Navy, and also the AV-8B Plus, when they were incorporated into the Squadrons in all the exercises in which the Spanish Navy participated periodically: ALFEX – exercises of the old Navy Alpha Group; SINKEX – in which the sinking of a disused ship was carried out; TAPON – a multinational exercise led by Spain, based in the Strait of Gibraltar; EOLO – an exercise in the Mediterranean led by Italy; ILES D'OR – an exercise led by France; NORTHERN LIGHT – an exercise led by the United Kingdom, and others of great significance such as LINKED SEAS, SHARP SPEAR, DISPLAY DETERMINATION, DYNAMIC MIX and STRONG RESOLVE. All these maneuvers have allowed the Spanish Harrier II aircraft to operate in areas such as the North Sea, the area of the Atlantic between the Canary Islands, Madera and mainland Spain, and the Mediterranean, facing all types of surface ships and a great variety of combat aircraft of allied nations. The Ninth Squadron gained experience in this manner on the different types of missions it was able to carry out, such as those of the air defense of the Fleet, armed reconnaissance, attacks on surface ships and land targets, helicopter escort and CAS (close

▶ A Harrier pilot aboard the *Príncipe de Asturias* aircraft carrier giving the thumbs up to the aircraft director, who has just given him the data sheet for take-off, during the *LINKED SEAS* exercise in May 1993. *(Luis Díaz-Bedia Astor)*

▼ An AV-8B taking off, at the moment of leaving the Ski-jump on the *Príncipe de Asturias*. The aircraft director is indicating that the next aircraft should undertake pre-take-off tests. The photo was taken during an exercise at the end of 1997. *(Luis Díaz-Bedia Astor)*

A recently landed aircraft and another nearing the carrier for landing, after completing a mission, during the *ALFEX 02/99* exercise. *(Luis Díaz-Bedia Astor)*

aerial support) to the Marine Corps. Particularly valuable, as far as the air defense and surface ship attack missions are concerned, was the information provided to the Harrier pilots by the interception controllers of the *Paqueteras*, as the SH-3D version of the AEW (Airborne Early Warning) of the Fifth Aeronaval Squadron are otherwise known.

Additionally they collaborated with TEAR (Marine Corps of the Spanish Navy) in practice CAS procedures in the Sierra del Retín training camp, as well as detachments from the Manises airbase to carry out shooting exercises in the Caudé firing range, until its closure, and from the Zaragoza airbase to shoot on the Las Bardenas firing range. Both at Sierra del Retín and Las Bardenas they performed numerous target-setting exercises with lasers, either with advanced control equipment on land or on board helicopters of the Third or Sixth Aeronaval Squadrons.

They also carried out frequent DACT (Dissimilar Air Combat Training) with different Air Force jet units to undertake mutual training in aerial combat against different types of aircraft. Particularly beneficial was combat with the F-18, the Mirage III until it was taken out of service, and the Mirage F-1, as they allowed squadrons to develop tactics against planes with radar, however pilots also showed great interest in

Lieutenant Manuel Rodríguez Giner, aboard the 01-903, above the Montes de León mountain range on February 3, 2000, during a navigation flight from Rota to Santiago de Compostela. *(Luis Díaz-Bedia Astor)*

collaborating with the F-5 of Talavera and with the C-101, especially when these formed part of the Ala 21 or Morón.

Harrier II aircraft participated regularly in Air Force exercises such as DAPEX, DAGA, SIRIO and AQUARIO. In these they undertook air defense missions, just like any Air Force fighter unit, and also attack missions, integrated on many occasions in units which also formed part of the veteran F-4 Phantom, the F-18 and Mirage F-1. They also took part on many occasions in

the electronic warfare NUBE GRIS exercise, whose first phase was developed at Los Llanos airbase.

The fact that the probe for in-flight refueling on the *Bravo* was retractable gave it more flexibility than the *Alfa* – which had a fixed version which had to be fitted just for refueling and then removed thereby affecting its flying characteristics. Since the creation of the Ninth Squadron the Harrier II aircraft has carried out a large number of collaborations for in-flight refueling with the KC-

130 of the Air Force Ala 35 and Squadron VR-122 Med Riders of the U.S. Navy, when it was based in Rota, as well as the Boeing 707 of Group 45. For some years the Harriers were included in the in-flight refueling flights planned by the Air Force for the training of its fighter and attack units.

Harrier aircraft are in great demand for collaborations for surface ship anti-aircraft training, not only by the Spanish Navy, but also by other allied countries who take advantage of travelling through Spanish coastal waters to undertake PASSEX ex-

The same day and the same flight as the previous photograph, passing over Santa Eugenia de Ribeira on the Arosa inlet. *(Luis Díaz-Bedia Astor)*

ercises. They have also been part of much collaboration with the Mistral missile unit of TEAR (Marine Corps of the Spanish Navy). Equally important are the exercises with the different units of the Antiaircraft Artillery Command of the Land Army, in which the AV-8B face missile batteries from Hawk, Aspide, Roland and Mistral and from 40/70 caliber cannons.

They have also undertaken exchanges with aerial units from other countries, amongst which are the F-18 Squadrons of the Canadian Air Force,

the Super Etendard of the French Navy, the Tornados of the German Navy and the Mirage 2000 of the Greek Air Force. In addition, they have undertaken exercises with Harriers of the U.S. Marines, the Royal Navy and the RAF, taking advantage of their detachment at Rota when the aircraft carriers on which they were boarded were at the ports of Rota or Cádiz.

Harrier II aircraft have also had the opportunity to operate from the decks of aircraft carriers from other countries such as the *John F. Kennedy* aircraft

carrier and the U.S. Marine *Nassau* and *Saipan* helicopter carriers, the British aircraft carriers *Ark Royal* and *Illustrious*, the Italian carrier *Giuseppe Garibaldi* and the Thai carrier *Chakrinaruebet*.

In terms of the participation of Harrier II in actual operations, during the Gulf War in 1991, the *Príncipe de Asturias* aircraft carrier remained in the Mediterranean from February 8th to March 8th, filling the space left by the units of the Sixth Fleet spread out across the area of operations.

From December 10th to 21st 1994 the *Príncipe de Asturias* was assigned to the Adriatic. It was the only occasion on which the Harrier Alfa and Bravo undertook flights in this area of operations, for unlike other European countries whose navies have aircraft carriers, there had never been a political will to keep a Spanish aircraft carrier and its On Board Air Group operating for a prolonged period of time in the area.

Unfortunately the use of the AV-8B by the Spanish Navy has not been without accidents. The three most serious have resulted in the loss of two pilots and a maintenance officer. On December 5, 1989 Lieutenant Raúl Pampillo Veiga disappeared in the Bay of Cádiz, aboard Aircraft 01-901, whilst carrying out an instrumental approach to the aerodrome of the Rota naval base. On 26 November 1993 Captain Ramón Martiño Rey, maintenance officer of the Squadron, was killed as a result of an accident which happened when tests were being carried out on aircraft 01-908. On February 19, 1998, the 01-902 had an accident at sea, close to Mazarrón, in which the pilot, Second Lieutenant Angel Marco Hernández, lost his life.

The Night Attack

The United States Marine Corps needed an airplane that could operate at night at low altitude, so that it could support its land forces twenty-four hours a day. For this reason the development

► Lieutenant Angel Saíz Padilla carrying out a reconnaissance flight off the coast of the Portuguese island of Madeira during *LINKED SEAS 2000* exercise. *(Luis Díaz-Bedia Astor)*

▼ The *Príncipe de Asturias* maneuvering in the port of Las Palmas in Gran Canaria to go out to sea on November 29, 1999, during *ALFEX-SINKEX 99* exercise. On the Ski-jump is an AV-8B and on deck three SH-3D helicopters can be made out, the second of which is the Alerta Temprana version. *(Luis Díaz-Bedia Astor)*

► A stationary aircraft before crossing the deck of the *Príncipe de Asturias* for take-off during the *ALFEX 02/99* exercise. *(Luis Díaz-Bedia Astor)*

▼ During the *ALFEX 02/99* exercise, in June of the same year, a commanding officer of the Ninth Squadron spraying the engine of an AV-8B with fresh water, after its landing on board the Príncipe de Asturias, with the aim of avoiding corrosion caused by the salt residue left on the aircraft when they undertake flights over the sea. *(Luis Díaz-Bedia Astor)*

of the *Night Attack* version was started from a modified aircraft in 1987. Two years later the first mass-produced aircraft was airborne, bringing the total number of Harrier II aircraft to 167. This version differed from the basic aircraft mainly in the NAVFLIR (Navigation Forward Looking Infra Red) located in the nose, larger sight HUD, a cockpit that was compatible with the use of night vision goggles – all the indicator lights are green – and a digital map on an additional multifunction screen in the cockpit. It had an F-402-RR-408 engine, more powerful than the 406, larger LERX, as well as additional chaff and flare dispensers in the upper part of the fuselage.

As far as the RAF was concerned, it signed, in 1988, a purchase order for thirty-four new GR7 aircraft, the British version of the *Night Attack*, to replace the GR3 aircraft at Wittering. The operating squadrons began to take delivery of them in 1990, and by 1996 all the GR5 and GR5A aircraft had been converted to the GR7 version.

The AV-8B Plus

The idea of a Harrier with radar came about in 1988 with the request of the U.S. Marine Corps for a modernized AV-8B that could carry out land attack missions by day and night even in adverse weather conditions. For their part, the Italian and Spanish Navies wanted an aircraft that, as well as

The first Harrier Plus on one of its initial flights. On the nose can be seen the flags of the three nations participating in the development program: Spain, the United States and Italy. It is easy to see the difference between the front cold nozzles and the hot ones behind. *(Boeing Photo)*

air-to-ground missions could carry out an efficient aerial defense of a naval force. The governments of the three nations signed an agreement in 1990 for the development of a new version of the Harrier, which would be undertaken by the McDonnell Douglas Company.

The maiden flight of the new aircraft took place on September 22, 1992. In the same year an agreement was signed for the production of the Harrier II Plus. On March 17, 1993 the first manufactured plane took to the air, and deliveries to the U.S. Marine Corps began in June of the same year. For the Marines the program meant not only the purchase of twenty-seven newly-built aircraft, but the remanufacturing of the AV-8B aircraft in service as well. The Italian Navy, which had requested sixteen aircraft, began to take delivery of them in 1994 and in November of the same year the first assessments were carried out on board the *Giuseppe Garibaldi*.

The AV-8B Plus in the Spanish Navy

In 1990 Spain accepted the invitation from McDonnell Douglas, which would later be taken over by Boeing, to join the Harrier II Plus program with the United States and Italy. The purchase order for eight aircraft was confirmed in 1993 and it was agreed that the final assembly of the aircraft for Spain would be carried out by CASA at its production facilities in San Pablo, Seville. The first of these, the

An AV-8B Plus in flight over the Mediterranean at the end of 1997, during an exercise with the NATO *STANAVFORLANT* (Standing Naval Force Atlantic Permanent). *(Luis Díaz-Bedia Astor)*

01-914, undertook its first landing at the Rota naval base on December 11th 1995, where it undertook stationary flight tests before being delivered to the Spanish Navy. It joined the list of Spanish Navy aircraft on January 30, 1996 and was delivered to Rota on May 24. The rest of the aircraft arrived at Rota during the following months with the final delivery being the 01-921, on July 1997, becoming active in the Spanish Navy on September 7 of the same year.

In addition to the purchase of these aircraft it was decided to remanufacture the EAV-8B to the Plus model, although unfortunately budget difficulties only allowed for the inclusion of five aircraft in the program. For this reason the Ninth Squadron will keep four *Day Attack* aircraft, which may be the last ones remaining in service in the world, although currently the possibility of converting them to the *Night Attack* version is being looked into, as the U.S. Marine Corps has included all its AV-8B aircraft in the remanufacturing program.

The incorporation of the AV-8B Plus means an enormous qualitative jump in terms of the capabilities of the Spanish Fleet for aerial defense and the hold of naval power on land twenty-four hours a day. This model can already be considered a true fighter, as it is fitted with an APG-65, the same radar as the F-18, with air-to-air and air-to-surface capacity. The Plus also integrates the air-to-air radar-guided AMRAAM missile, with a range of around twenty miles. This missile receives information from the aircraft's radar to determine the future position of

A Harrier Plus from the VMA-223 *Bulldogs* Squadron of the U.S. Marine Corps carrying out a closed turn. For armaments it has four Mk-82 bombs with fins for low-drag and GAU-12 cannon. *(Boeing Photo)*

the target and to carry out an inertial guide for the first phase of the flight, activating its own radar in the final phase, and giving the enemy little reaction time, as it is only detected when it is already right on top of the target.

The Plus is an impressive night attack aircraft due to its FLIR, navigation system with integrated GPS, and an optimized cockpit for the pilot to use NVG (night vision goggles). In 1996 the Ninth Squadron converted the first Spanish fighter plane to use NVG, which increases the dim natural light to allow for a view of the outside, even at low

altitudes of sixty meters, to decide if conditions are favorable. The Plus, like the *Night Attack*, also incorporates the infrared AGM-65 Maverick missile, which allows for improved precision and attacking distance, day and night, against sea and land surface targets.

The incorporation of the Plus benefits the preparation and tactics of the pilots of Spanish Harriers. On the one hand they are no longer blind in the air-to-air environment and can measure up to the most advanced fighters, and on the other they are able to operate at

night from the *Príncipe de Asturias* and carry out missions which were unthinkable until their inclusion. They are also pioneers in the *en visual* night landing when the aircraft carrier is totally obscured, achieving greater flexibility for on board recoveries. Since their arrival the Plus aircraft have participated together with the *Day Attack* aircraft in all the exercises that the Ninth Squadron has taken part in.

Collaborations with foreign units continue to be carried out. On one of these, on January 28, 1998, in which the two aircraft of the Ninth Squadron detached to the Landivisiau French air naval base, a Plus carried out the first refueling of a Harrier by a Super Etendard with a refueling probe, which increases the possibilities of combined operations between the fighter naval aircraft of both nations.

On February 12, 1999 a Plus landed on the landing platform dock of the *Galicia* to certify the ship's deck for flight operations with Harriers. The *Galicia* and its sister ship the *Castilla* could be used as alternatives for the landing of Harriers if necessary. In March of the same year the radar simulator AV-8B Plus *SRPlus* made by the Spanish company INDRA went into service. This simulator does not include the complete cockpit and does not have a visual system showing the outside, it simply shows information of the on board systems. Its main mission is the formation and training in basic radar operations, air-to-air and air-to-surface operations, aerial interception and operations with reduced radar. In April/May a new landmark in the training of pilots of the Ninth Squadron was reached when two of them undertook the NATO TLP (Tactical Leadership Program). In October the Plus aircraft used GBU-12 laser guided bombs for the first time. In 2001 two laser and infrared designator Litening II pods were acquired, which were flight-tested between July 2 and 6 of that year. These pods gave the Squadron self-sufficiency when designating bombing targets with the laser guided GBU-12.

On July 31, 2003 the first two remanufactured aircraft, with the new numerals 01-923 and 01-924 were delivered to the Spanish Navy at Cherry

The frigate *Extremadura* turning around the starboard of the *Príncipe de Asturias*, on whose deck a Harrier II Plus can be seen while the nose of another is situated on the elevator during some exercises in 1998.
(Luis Díaz-Bedia Astor)

One of the remodeled Plus aircraft delivered to the Spanish Navy on June 31, 2003 at Cherry Point, North Carolina, refueling whilst in-flight during the Atlantic crossing that it undertook at the beginning of August of that year.
(Luis Cabeza Barrios)

Point. Three pilots took it in turns to carry out the stages of the Atlantic crossing between August 7 and 9, 2003, with stops in Goose Bay, Canada, and Keflavik, Iceland, aided by an Air Force TK-17, 707, tanker aircraft.

In September of the same year the new AV-8B Plus simulator was delivered to the Spanish Navy, built by the Spanish company Indra, representing a new step forward in the training of Spanish Harrier pilots, who would then not have

to transfer to Cherry Point to undertake the Plus adaptation course.

In terms of participation in actual operations, the Harrier Plus and Day Attack took part in the Romeo

Sierra operation for the recovery of Perejil Island, from July 16 to July 20, 2002, staying in the air ready to carry out CAS missions. At the beginning of March 2003 the *Príncipe de Asturias*, with ten Harrier II aircraft on board, went to sea to take part in the GRUFLEX exercise in the Western Mediterranean. Although there was speculation about possible orders to go to the Persian Gulf to participate in the Iraqi Freedom operation, the Spanish government decided not to include the aircraft carrier among the ships sent to the area.

The use of the Plus by the Spanish Navy has also not escaped accidents. On April 21, 2003 the 01-921 was lost during an air-to-air training flight with F-18 aircraft of the Ala 12 in the Gulf of Cádiz. The pilot, Lieutenant José María Fernández de la Puente, ejected and was picked up by a helicopter from the Third Squadron.

The Spanish Navy achieves a two-seater

Although from the beginning the Ninth Squadron had a modern flight simulator, it always understood

Aircraft 923 and 924 in formation with the TK-17 of the Air force that accompanied them and provided fuel during the Atlantic crossing that they undertook between August 7 and 9 of 2003.
(Luis Cabana Barrios)

the importance of acquiring a two-seat training aircraft for the instruction of new pilots and the regularization of procedures. It eventually reached an agreement with Boeing for the acquisition, through leasing, of the TAV-8B – BUNO 162747 – belonging to this company, whose first flight in the United States had taken place in October 1988. On February 12, 2001 it took delivery of the disassembled aircraft at the Rota naval base and on 29th of the same month it was included on the Spanish Navy Aircraft List under number 01-922. Personnel from the CASA production facilities at San Pablo, Seville, undertook the modification, assembly and adjustment work, and on May 7 the aircraft undertook its first test flight. With the acquisition of this aircraft, the officers who had completed the naval pilot course in the United States could start to undertake initial instruction actually in the Squadron rather than with the VMAT-203 Squadron of the Marines as they had been doing previously.

Flights in a Harrier

Perhaps the first impression that a Spanish Navy pilot has when finally completing the Naval Aviator course in the U.S. and beginning to fly the Harrier are of the power of its engine, which is clearly demonstrated by the acceleration that it achieves during takeoff, strong enough to glue someone physically to the seat, as well as the peculiar sensation of a VSTOL flight. Used to

A *Day Attack* and a *Plus*, in closed formation with their leader, returning to Rota after a training flight over the province of Huelva, in January 2000. *(Luis Díaz-Bedia Astor)*

The author in closed formation with the leader during training flight over the province of Huelva, in the summer of 1993. *(collection of Luis Díaz-Bedia Astor)*

landings in the old TA-4J Skyhawk – for the more veteran pilots – or in the T-45 Goshawk, the fact of reducing the speed of a fighter plane until it stops in the air seems an unnatural concept. But little by little the pilot begins to like it and becomes accustomed to the great variety of landings and takeoffs which gives a greater flexibility for flight operations, and above all, allows the Harrier, without the need for hooks and brake ropes, to land on board a sea vessel. On a stationary flight the pilot governs the aircraft in a way similar to a helicopter, although the lift is given by the outgoing jet from adjustable nozzles controlled by the corresponding extra handle in the cockpit which are directed towards the ground, and the control of the movements in the three shafts is achieved thanks to the small outflows of air in the nose, tail and wing ends.

The landings on board the *Príncipe de Asturias* always increase the adrenalin rush for the pilot as

A *Plus* and a *Day Attack* during a training flight over the province of Huelva in April 2000. *(Luis Díaz-Bedia Astor)*

Lieutenant Luis López Herrera flying over the province of Granada on board the 01-905, returning from an exercise with an anti-air artillery unit of the Land Army in the province of Murcia, after having refueled at the San Javier air base, on February 9, 2000. *(Luis Díaz-Bedia Astor)*

▶ A Plus on the deck of the *Príncipe de Asturias* aircraft carrier after landing on board. *(Luis Díaz-Bedia Astor)*

the vertical take off is the only option and a failure or breakdown would mean trying to get to an alternative airport within a manageable distance or otherwise not being able to land. Without a doubt the most critical landings are those at night, in which the change from conventional to stationary flight is undertaken without any external visual references and the direction of the flight deck on the aircraft carrier cannot easily be distinguished until it is very close.

On a conventional flight the Harrier behaves in a way very similar to other aircraft, although it does have certain special features: its large air inflows, conceived of for VSTOL, are not exactly aerodynamic, making it a relatively slow aircraft, unable to pass the sound barrier.

The nozzles, although conceived of mainly for a VSTOL flight, can be used in air-to-air combat to make very tight turns; these can help to achieve the optimum firing angle for the Sidewinder missile or cannon and as a last resort maneuver to avoid enemy fire. In any case the use of the nozzles in combat must be carried out carefully, as the aircraft loses so much energy that afterwards it is difficult to recover it without using the afterburners.

The AV-8B is an excellent strike aircraft, with a magnificent firing system that allows for the identification of targets by means of a video system or through laser designation from the land or from the air.

Although its load capacity is less than that of the F-18, it has a wide array of air-to-surface weapons, including free-fall bombs, retarded bombs (dropped at low altitude), laser guided bombs, rockets and 25mm cannons.

Back view of an AV-8B aircraft in the parking area of the Zaragoza airbase during the detachment arming in March 2000. The particular shape of the wings and the stabilizers can be seen, as well as the characteristic landing gear composed of the nose gear with a wheel, main gear with two *outriggers*, one on each wing. The protuberances at the ends of the wings correspond to the *puffers* of the *Reaction Control System* to control the warping of a VSTOL flight. On the far outside weapons stations there are LAU-7 launchers on each one, from which hang the Sidewinder missiles, halfway between there are two ITER with three Mk-76 exercise bombs each, and inside two ITER without bombs. In the cone of the tail the back navigation light can be seen in the centre and two radar warning aerials. Behind the main gear is the air brake which stays in a spread out position when the gear is down. *(Luis Díaz-Bedia Astor)*

► Personnel of the weapons division of the Ninth Squadron installing a Sidewinder captive missile on the side of an AV-8B. The captive missile cannot be fired without a jet engine, but it has the same infrared seeker head as a war missile and shows the same information in the HUD before firing, and therefore is indispensable for the training of pilots in the air-to-air environment. *(Luis Díaz-Bedia Astor)*

▼ An AV-8B aircraft at the Rota naval base with part of its armament range. In the external stations of each side are both AIM-9L/I Sidewinder missiles hung with LAU-7 launchers, on the immediate right is a 2.75 in. four-rocket launcher and on the left an ITER – a device capable of housing three bombs – with a Mk-106 exercise bomb, whilst in each internal station a BR-250 bomb is hung. In front of the aircraft there is the GAU-12 cannon and munitions holder, with 300 rounds, which are installed in the left and right ventral areas respectively, replacing the LIDS. On one side is a radar guided AMRAAM (*Advanced Medium Range Air to Air Missile*). In the nose there is also the radome of the APG-65 radar, as well as the NAVFLIR. In front of the cockpit the weather vane which allows the pilot to gain information about the direction of the wind when undertaking vertical landings and take-offs can clearly be seen. In the engine's left air inlet the retracted in-flight refueling probe can be made out. *(Luis Díaz-Bedia Astor)*

Its air-to-air capacity is limited however, as it lacks radar and is armed only with a Sidewinder missile and the cannon, which limits it to short distances in combat.

The AV-8B Plus can be considered a true fighter aircraft. The way in which the Harrier pilots fly in the air-to-air environment has changed significantly since the inclusion of this aircraft. The APG-65 radar allows not only for the acquisition and pursuit of aerial targets, but also the ability to react to threat much more efficiently. With the integration of the AMRAAM they can compare themselves favorably to aircraft which until recently had been considered superior. The Plus is also an aircraft with an excellent nocturnal capability. The FLIR and above all the NVG have totally changed night flights, allowing the pilots the possibility of flying with visibility; these systems together with the incorporation of the Maverick missile have substantially changed the possibilities of surface attack for this aircraft.

Perhaps the negative features of the Harrier II are that it only has one engine, making it more vulnerable to breakdowns and faults, tied to the fact that its particular capacity for stationary flight requires systems that complicate its operation and can lead to additional breakdowns.

To conclude, it should be emphasized that all the pilots who have flown these aircraft feel proud for belonging to a unique group in fighter and strike aviation, that of VSTOL, and for having had first

▶ The author checking the ANVIS-9 night vision goggles. El Plus, as well as having the advantage of radar and FLIR, has an optimized cockpit for the use of goggles, which allows one to fly at low altitude at night, considerably increasing its operative possibilities. *(collection Luis Díaz-Bedia Astor)*

▼ The author in ascent during a flight in the Gulf of Cádiz, in March 2000. *(Luis Díaz-Bedia Astor)*

hand experience of forming part of the history of the Harrier, which without a doubt occupies a distinguished place in the world of aviation and can be considered one of the most extraordinary aircraft of all time.

Take-off of an AV-8B aboard the *Príncipe de Asturias*, seen from the cockpit of the leader of the formation, who has just taken off. The symbols of the HUD, showing the pilot different data on the aircraft, can be seen. In this case, to the left, there is a speed over the air mass of thirty knots – as the aircraft is stationary it indicates the wind on deck – an attack angle of the wings on the air flow of 7.0, a land speed of seventeen knots – the speed of the ship – 29% of the engine revolutions, the expulsion temperature of gases of 515º C. To the right the Flaps angle of 4º, an angle of rotation of the nozzles of 12º, the time of 18.04 GMT – the seconds cannot be seen due to the position of the camera – a distance to the TACAN from the ship of 0.1 miles and a rhythm of descent of 500 ft. a minute – due to the movement of the ship on the waves – above that there is something indicating a height of 10 ft. above the deck, but this cannot be seen clearly. Due to the light the direction cannot be seen in the upper part. On top of the ski-jump there is the artificial horizon and a little higher up the vector speed which indicates which direction the aircraft should go in – when the speed is more than sixty knots – and the rhythm of ascent and descent for a speed less than sixty knots – lower down the witch's hat can be seen, which gives an indication of the angle of the nose. In the lower part the ball is practically in the center, showing that the tail rudder is adjusted in such a way that the longitudinal axis of the aircraft is centered with the forward direction over the air mass. The 5º and 10º marks can also be seen on the low nose.
(*Luis Díaz-Bedia Astor*)

At the end of the *LINKED SEAS* exercise, on May 16, 2000, a Gato – AB-212 helicopter of the Third Aircraft Squadron – and two Cobras meet at their landing points on the flight deck of the *Príncipe de Asturias*, before carrying out a crossing to the Rota naval base, whilst a Morsa of the Fifth Squadron is parked to the portside of the island. The photo is taken from the cockpit of an AV-8B. *(Luis Díaz-Bedia Astor)*

AV-8B / B Plus in the Spanish Navy

Bureau Number	Old Aircraft	Registrations in effect	Registration	In service	Out of service
163010	01-901	VA-11	VA.1A-13	6-10-1987	27-02-1990 (Accident)
163011	01-902	VA-12	VA.1A-14	6-10-1987	5-05-1998 (Accident)
163012	01-903	VA-13	VA.1A-15	6-10-1987	
163013	01-904	VA-14	VA.1A-16	2-11-1987	6-04-2001 (Retrofit)
163014	01-905	VA-15	VA.1A-17	2-11-1987	6-04-2001 (Retrofit)
163015	01-906	VA-16	VA.1A-18	2-11-1987	2-07-2002 (Retrofit)
163016	01-907	VA-17	VA.1A-19	17-05-1988	
163017	01-908	VA-18	VA.1A-32	17-05-1988	26-11-1993 (Accident)
163018	01-909	VA-19	VA.1A-20	17-05-1988	
163019	01-910	VA-20	VA.1A-21	31-08-1988	2-07-2002 (Retrofit)
163020	01-911	VA-21	VA.1A-22	15-09-1988	
163021	01-912	VA-22	VA.1A-23	15-09-1988	2-07-2002 (Retrofit)
165028	01-914	VA.1B-24		30-01-1996	
165029	01-915	VA.1B-25		26-05-1996	
165030	01-916	VA.1B-26		19-06-1996	
165031	01-917	VA.1B-27		12-09-1996	
165032	01-918	VA.1B-28		22-03-1997	
165033	01-919	VA.1B-29		7-03-1997	
165034	01-920	VA.1B-30		10-07-1997	
165035	01-921	VA.1B-31		16-10-1997	
162747	01-922	VA.1B-33		29-02-2002	
165652	01-923	VA.1B-35		23-08-2003	
165653	01-924	VA.1B-36		23-08-2003	

• Aircraft 01-903, 01-907, 01-909 and 01-911 will not be remanufactured to the Plus model, although the possibility of its transformation into the Night Attack version are being looked into.
• Total flight hours up to September 30, 2003 = 35,895

AV-8B / B Plus Technical Specifications

Dimensions

Wingspan	30.33 ft, all versions
Length	AV-8B: 46.33 ft, AV-8B Plus: 47.75 ft, TAV-8B: 50.53 ft
Height	AV-8B: 11.65 ft, AV-8B Plus: 11.65 ft, TAV-8B: 13.09 ft
Distance between wing gear	17 ft, all versions

Weight of Aircraft

Weight without fuel or water	AV-8B: 12.977 lbs, AV-8B Plus: 14.755 lbs, TAV-8B: 14.178 lbs
Maximum landing weight	32.000 lbs, both versions
Maximum take-off weight	26.000 lbs, both versions

Wing Area   230 ft² –21.367m²–

Power and Lift

	AV-8B: F402-RR-406 Pegasus engine
Thrust	With water: 21.550 lbs, Dry: 20.280 lbs, AV-8B Plus: F402-RR-408 Pegasus engine
Thrust	With water: 23.400 lbs, Dry: 22.200 lbs

Range

with internal fuel	approx. 1h
with two external tanks	approx. 1h 30min.
with four external tanks	approx. 2h

Maximum Speed

AV-8B and AV-8B Plus	585 knots / 1 Mach
TAV-8B	550 knots / 0,9 Mach

Other

Maximum altitude	42.000 ft
Types of take-off and landing	Conventional, slow, rolling vertical (very slow), vertical.

Communications   2 ARC-182 or ARC-210 radios, both with VHF/UHF transmission/reception, and coding capacity via KY-58 equipment.

Armament

Air-to-air missiles:	Sidewinder AIM-9L/I, AMRAAM AIM-120
Air-to-surface missiles	Maverick AGM-65
Laser guided bombs	GBU-12
Free-fall bombs	Mk-82, Mk-83, BR-250, BR-500
Cluster bombs	Mk-20
Incendiary bombs	Mk-77
Rockets	5 in ZUNI, 2.75 in FFAR
Cannon	25 mm GAU-12 (air-to-air and air-to-surface)

Electronic Warfare Systems

Warning	AN/ALR-67
Electronic warfare pod	AN/ALQ-164
Chaff/flares dispenser	AN/ALE-39

Other Systems   TACAN, IFF. Inertial navigation system, with incorporated GPS in the case of the Plus. ARBS firing system in the AV-8B. APG-65 radar in the AV-8B Plus, NAVFLIR in the AV-8B Plus. Mission planning and automatic data entry system in the AV-8B Plus.

The *Príncipe de Asturias* aircraft carrier sailing in the Gulf of Cádiz in September 2003, with two AV-8B Plus parked to the rear. On the flight deck the line that serves as a reference for pilots for landings and take-offs can be seen. *(Luis Díaz-Bedia Astor)*

The Ninth Squadron of the Air force has been engaged in pilot exchange schemes with the U.S. Marine Corps. In this photo, Lieutenant Dan Duggan returns to the Zaragoza base after firing practice in Bardenas, in March 2000. The Pyrenees can be seen in the background. *(Luis Díaz-Bedia Astor)*

Aircraft AV-8B Plus in flight. Its sharp-pointed nose can be seen, housing the APG-65 radar, over which the NAVFLIR is overhanging. In the back section of the fuselage are two of the four side chaff/flares dispensers that the Plus has in addition to the two in the ventral area, which are the only ones the AV-8B has. *(Boeing Photo)*

The 01-922 aircraft, the two-seat TAV-8B of the Ninth Squadron, in the flight line of the Rota Naval Base. The massive nose section can be seen, whose aerodynamic effect has had to be compensated for with a larger resistant area. The weather vanes showing both pilots the information about the wind can be seen. In the nose the ARBS firing system lens can be seen. *(Luis Díaz-Bedia Astor)*

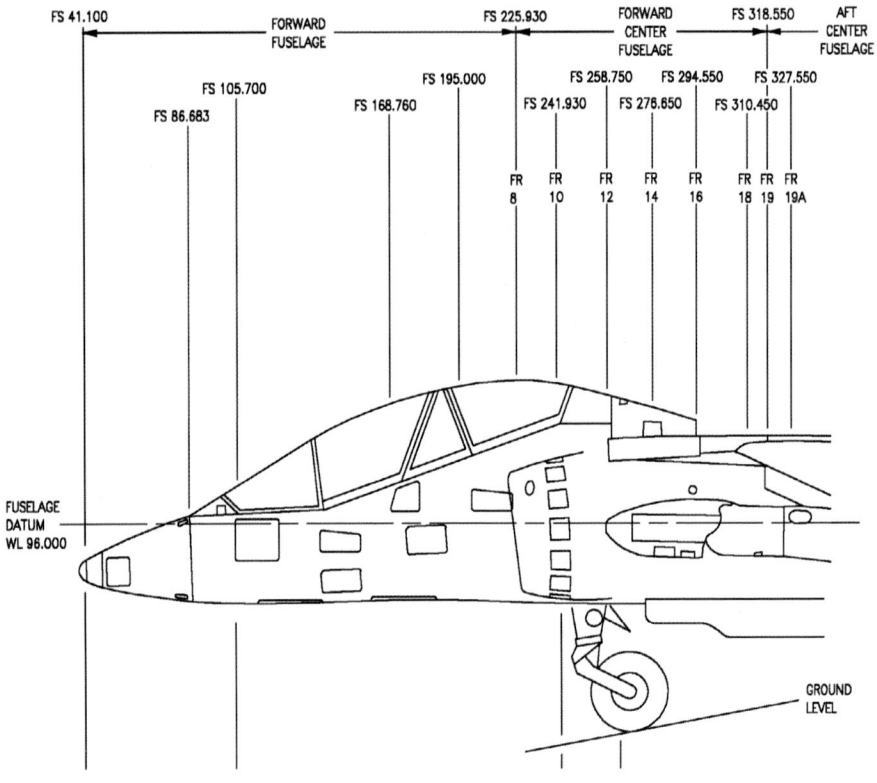

FS 41.100

FORWARD FUSELAGE

FS 225.930

FORWARD CENTER FUSELAGE

FS 318.550

AFT CENTER FUSELAGE

FS 105.700

FS 86.683

FS 195.000

FS 168.760

FS 258.750

FS 241.930

FS 276.650

FS 294.550

FS 327.550

FS 310.450

FR 8
FR 10
FR 12
FR 14
FR 16
FR 18
FR 19
FR 19A

FUSELAGE DATUM WL 96.000

GROUND LEVEL

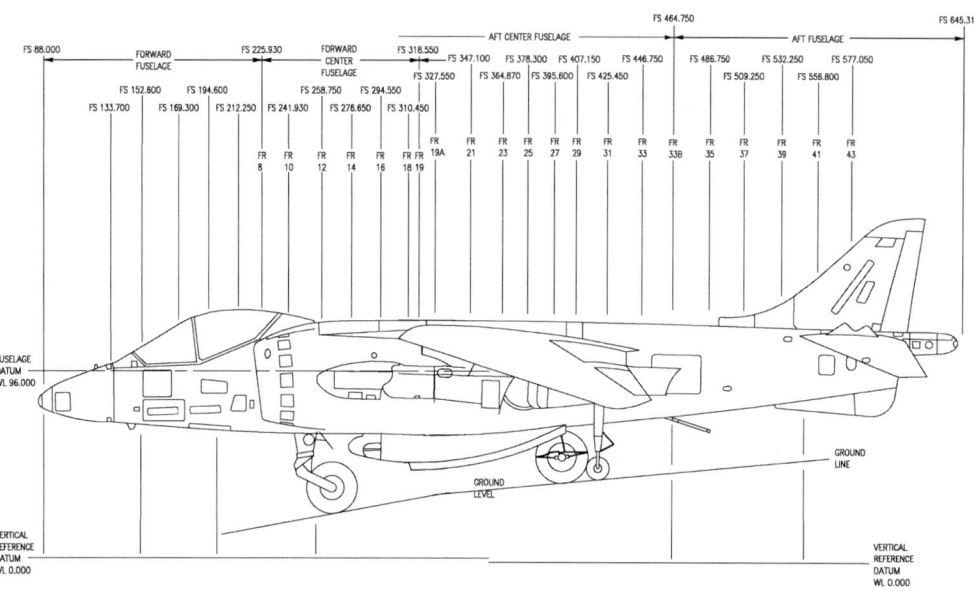

FS 88.000

FORWARD FUSELAGE

FS 225.930

FORWARD CENTER FUSELAGE

FS 318.550

AFT CENTER FUSELAGE

FS 464.750

AFT FUSELAGE

FS 645.312

FS 347.100
FS 378.300
FS 407.150
FS 446.750
FS 486.750
FS 532.250
FS 577.050

FS 152.800
FS 194.600
FS 258.750
FS 294.550
FS 327.550
FS 364.870
FS 395.600
FS 425.450
FS 509.250
FS 556.800

FS 133.700
FS 169.300
FS 212.250
FS 241.930
FS 276.650
FS 310.450

FR 8
FR 10
FR 12
FR 14
FR 16
FR 18
FR 19
FR 19A
FR 21
FR 23
FR 25
FR 27
FR 29
FR 31
FR 33
FR 33B
FR 35
FR 37
FR 39
FR 41
FR 43

FUSELAGE DATUM WL 96.000

GROUND LINE

GROUND LEVEL

VERTICAL REFERENCE DATUM WL 0.000

VERTICAL REFERENCE DATUM WL 0.000

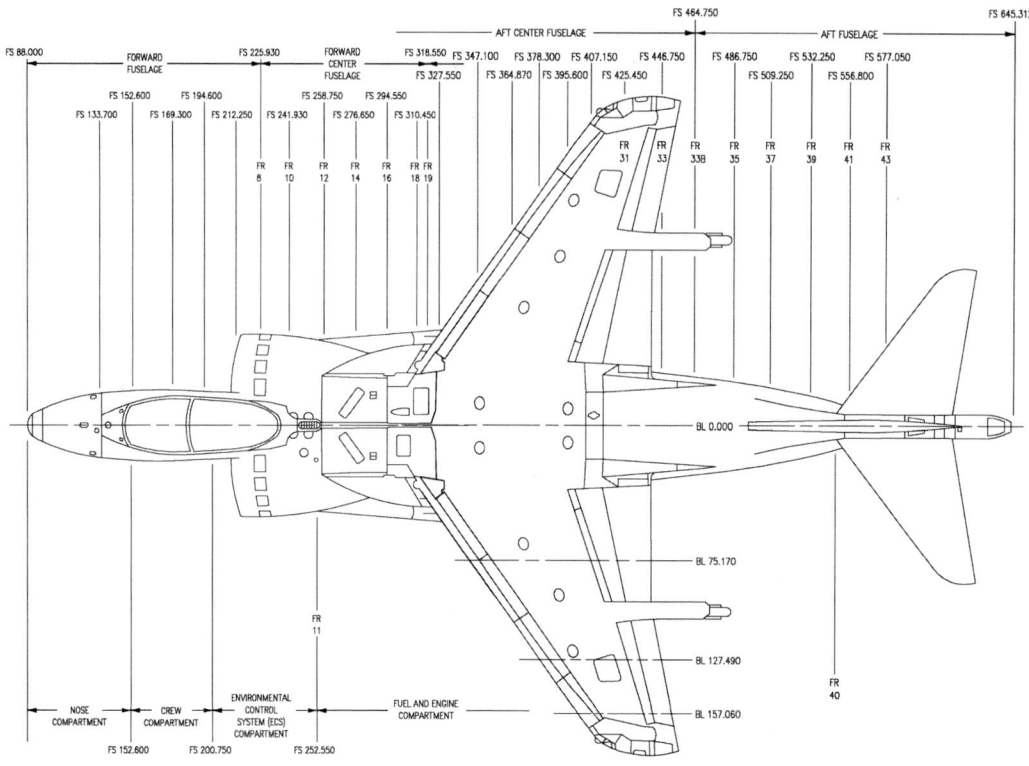

FS 88.000

FORWARD FUSELAGE

FS 225.930

FORWARD CENTER FUSELAGE

FS 318.550

AFT CENTER FUSELAGE

FS 464.750

AFT FUSELAGE

FS 645.312

FS 347.100
FS 378.300
FS 407.150
FS 446.750
FS 486.750
FS 532.250
FS 577.050

FS 152.600
FS 194.600
FS 258.750
FS 294.550
FS 327.550
FS 364.870
FS 395.600
FS 425.450
FS 509.250
FS 556.800

FS 133.700
FS 169.300
FS 212.250
FS 241.930
FS 276.650
FS 310.450

FR 8
FR 10
FR 12
FR 14
FR 16
FR 18
FR 19
FR 31
FR 33
FR 33B
FR 35
FR 37
FR 39
FR 41
FR 43

BL 0.000

BL 75.170

FR 11

BL 127.490

FR 40

BL 157.060

NOSE COMPARTMENT

CREW COMPARTMENT

ENVIRONMENTAL CONTROL SYSTEM (ECS) COMPARTMENT

FUEL AND ENGINE COMPARTMENT

FS 152.600

FS 200.750

FS 252.550

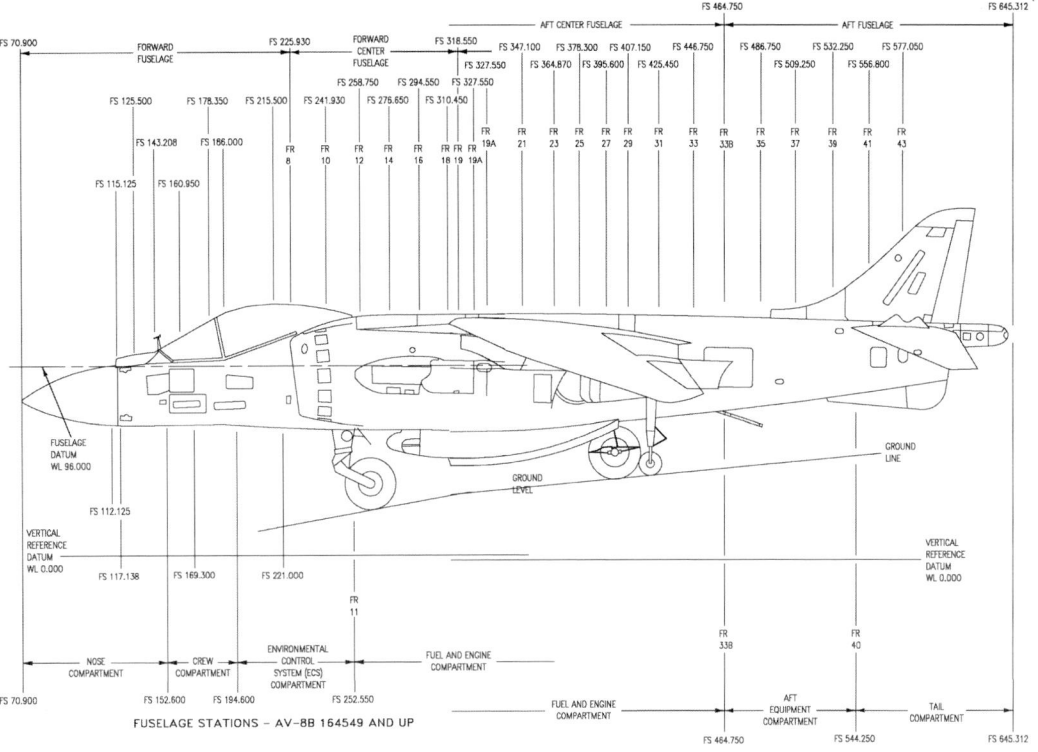

FS 464.750 FS 645.312

AFT CENTER FUSELAGE   AFT FUSELAGE

FS 70.900

FORWARD
FUSELAGE

FS 225.930   FORWARD
CENTER
FUSELAGE   FS 318.550

FS 347.100 FS 378.300 FS 407.150 FS 446.750
FS 327.550   FS 364.870 FS 395.600 FS 425.450   FS 486.750 FS 532.250 FS 577.050
FS 258.750 FS 294.550 FS 327.550   FS 509.250 FS 556.800

FS 125.500 FS 178.350 FS 215.500
FS 241.930 FS 276.650 FS 310.450

FS 143.208 FS 186.000

FR   FR   FR   FR   FR   FR FR FR   FR   FR   FR   FR   FR   FR   FR   FR   FR   FR
8   10   12   14   16   18 19 19A 21   23   25   27   29   31   33   33B 35   37   39   41   43

FS 115.125 FS 160.950

FS 112.125

FUSELAGE
DATUM
WL 96.000

GROUND
LINE

VERTICAL
REFERENCE
DATUM
WL 0.000

GROUND
LEVEL

VERTICAL
REFERENCE
DATUM
WL 0.000

FS 117.138   FS 169.300   FS 221.000

FR
11

FR
33B

FR
40

NOSE
COMPARTMENT

CREW
COMPARTMENT

ENVIRONMENTAL
CONTROL
SYSTEM (ECS)
COMPARTMENT

FUEL AND ENGINE
COMPARTMENT

FS 70.900

FS 152.600   FS 194.600

FS 252.550

FUEL AND ENGINE
COMPARTMENT

AFT
EQUIPMENT
COMPARTMENT

TAIL
COMPARTMENT

FS 464.750   FS 544.250   FS 645.312

FUSELAGE STATIONS – AV-8B 164549 AND UP

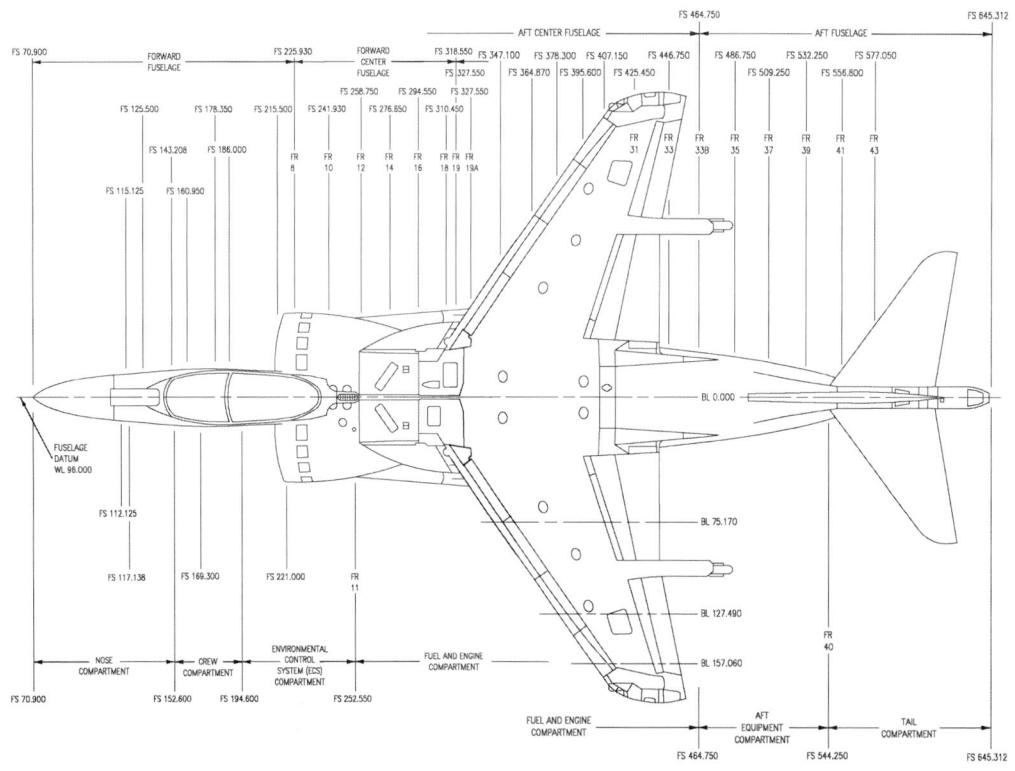

FS 464.750   FS 645.312

AFT CENTER FUSELAGE   AFT FUSELAGE

FS 70.900

FORWARD
FUSELAGE

FS 225.930   FORWARD
CENTER
FUSELAGE   FS 318.550   FS 347.100 FS 378.300 FS 407.150 FS 446.750
FS 327.550   FS 364.870 FS 395.600 FS 425.450   FS 486.750 FS 532.250 FS 577.050
FS 258.750 FS 294.550 FS 327.550   FS 509.250 FS 556.800

FS 125.500 FS 178.350 FS 215.500
FS 241.930 FS 276.650 FS 310.450

FS 143.208 FS 186.000

FR   FR   FR   FR   FR   FR FR FR   FR   FR   FR   FR   FR   FR   FR   FR
31   33   33B 35   37   39   41   43
8   10   12   14   16   18 19 19A

FS 115.125 FS 160.950

FS 112.125

BL 0.000

FUSELAGE
DATUM
WL 96.000

BL 75.170

FS 117.138   FS 169.300   FS 221.000

FR
11

BL 127.490

FR
40

NOSE
COMPARTMENT

CREW
COMPARTMENT

ENVIRONMENTAL
CONTROL
SYSTEM (ECS)
COMPARTMENT

FUEL AND ENGINE
COMPARTMENT

BL 157.060

FS 70.900

FS 152.600   FS 194.600

FS 252.550

FUEL AND ENGINE
COMPARTMENT

AFT
EQUIPMENT
COMPARTMENT

TAIL
COMPARTMENT

FS 464.750   FS 544.250   FS 645.312

AV-8B Plus: Cockpit and control panel

1. In-flight refueling lights. **5.** Control panel for electronic countermeasures. **8.** Landing verification panel. **14.** Empty panel. **15.** Manual fuel flow locking lever. **17.** Seat adjustment and exterior lights panel. **19.** Emergency battery for manual fuel control. **23.** Emergency gear battery. **24.** Take-off verification panel. **25.** Water injection and combat option engine control panel. **26.** Gear indicator lights. **30.** Main armament control panel. **31.** Emergency lights panel. **33.** ODU data monitor. **34.** UFC data control panel. **38.** Digital fuel gauge. **43.** Load stations control panel. **44.** Auxiliary attack angle gauge. **50.** Pedal position adjustment button. **51.** Systems control panel: radar, inertial, FLIR, mission computer, etc. **52.** Circuit breakers. **53.** Movement transducer. **54.** Stick. **58.** Auxiliary communications, navigation and IFF control panel. **59.** Cockpit lights control panel. **60.** Cockpit heat control panel. **63.** Video recorder. **64.** Pilot services panel: oxygen connection and anti-G suit. **65.** Exterior light panel. **66.** Fuel gauge control panel. **67.** Gases lever, nozzle control levers and parking brake. **68.** Stabilization system panel. **69.** Control panel and trimming indicator. **70.** Gear and flaps control panel. **72.** Emergency lights panel. **73.** Threat indicator lights panel. **75.** Hydraulic pressure gauge. **76.** Brake accumulator pressure indicator. **77.** Cockpit air pressure indicator. **79.** Magnetic needle. **81.** HUD (Head Up Display). **82.** Engine data indicator **83.** Left multifunction screen. **84.** Right multifunction screen. **85.** Analogue clock. **87.** Auxiliary gyroscope. **88.** Auxiliary speed gauge. **90.** Auxiliary ascent/descent rate indicator. **91.** Auxiliary turn rate indicator.

Second Lieutenant Cristóbal Peña carrying out tests in the cockpit of a Plus, in the hangar of the Ninth Squadron of the Air force. The right multifunction screen can be seen, on which the radar is usually shown. The HUD (Head Up Display) is covered with a protective cover, under which is the UFC (Up Front Control) which allows the pilot to input data in the mission computer during the flight. *(Luis Díaz-Bedia Astor)*

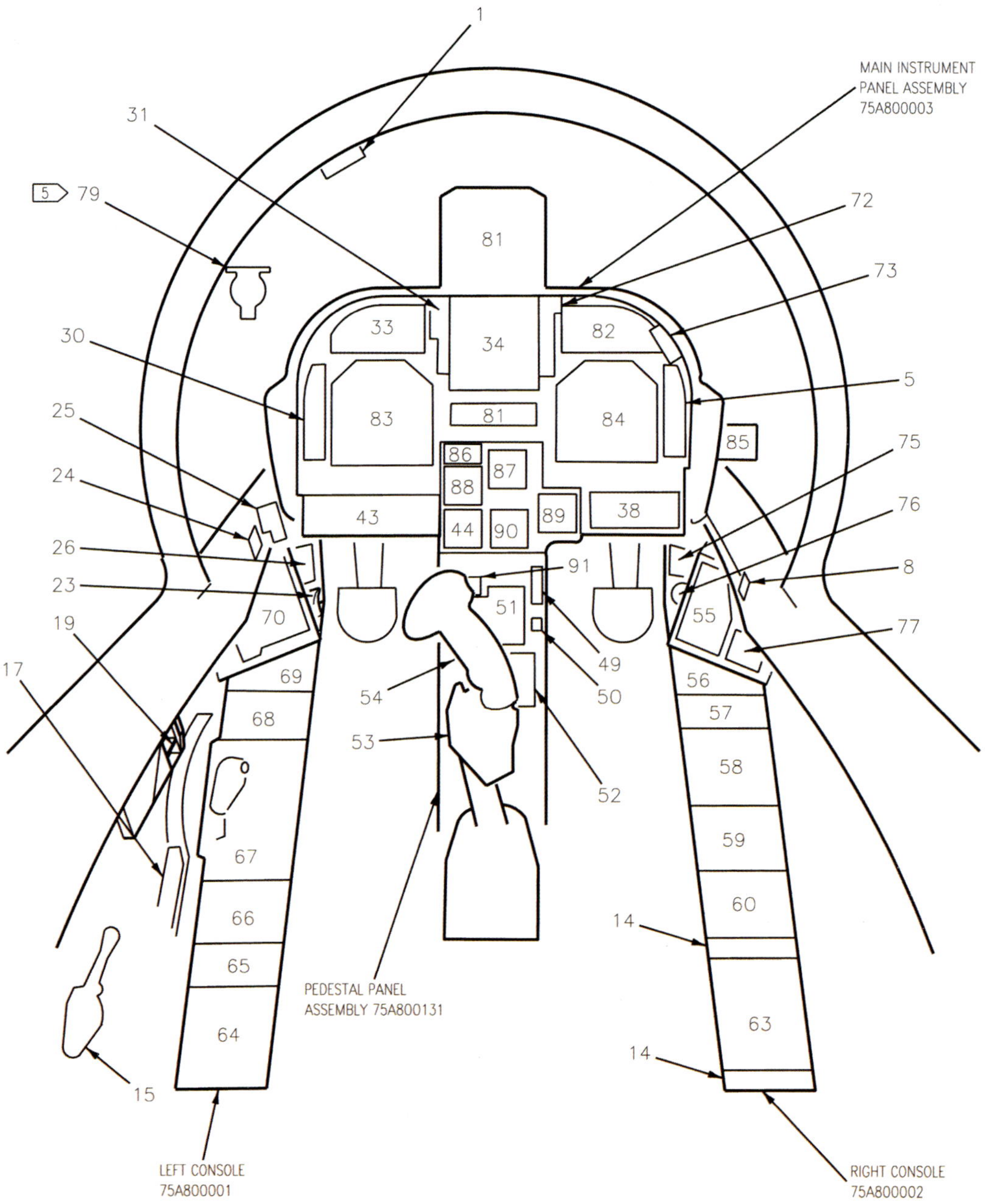

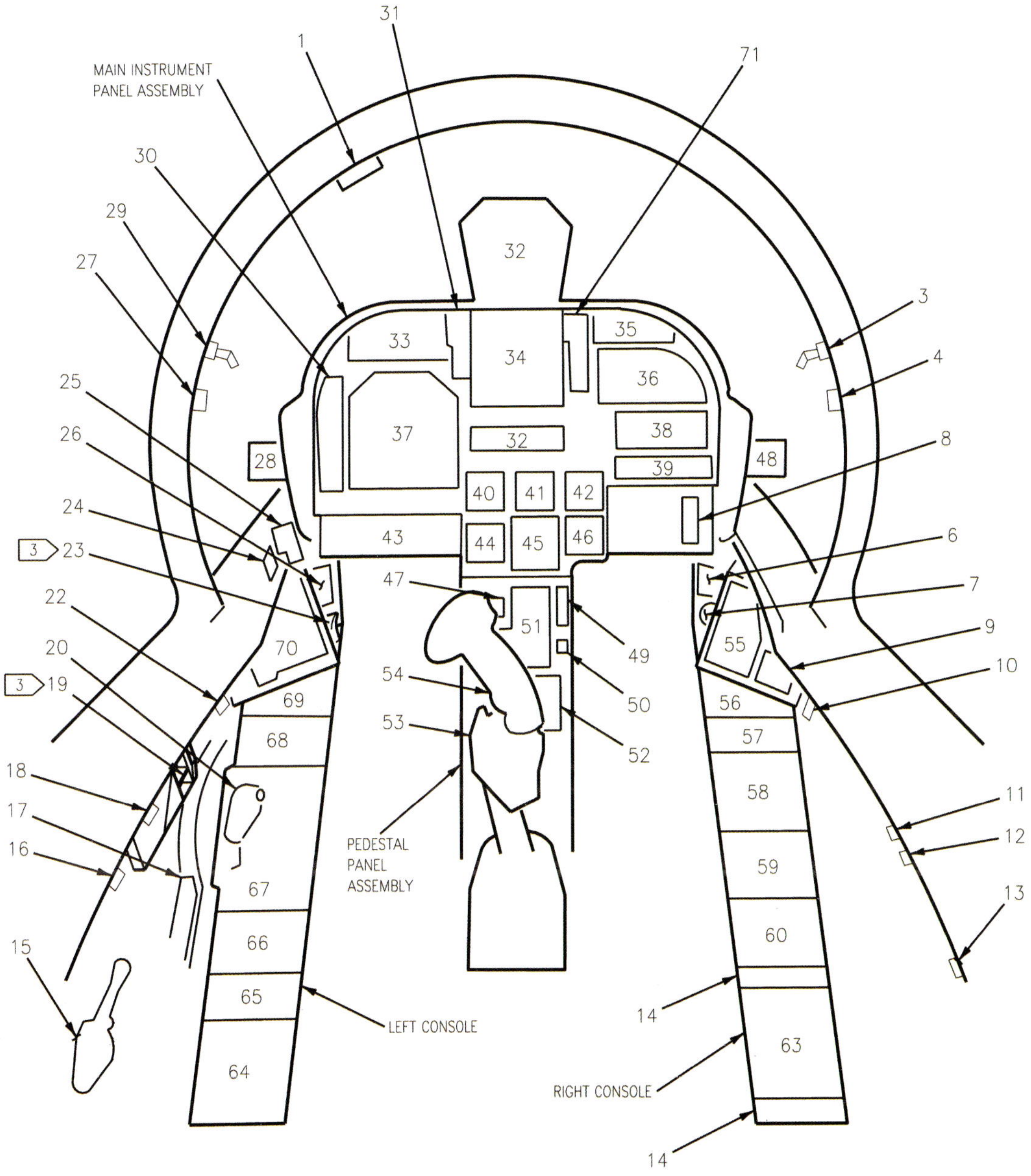

MAIN INSTRUMENT
PANEL ASSEMBLY

31

1

71

30

29

27

32

3

25

35

33

34

26

36

4

24

37

32

38

8

28

48

39

3 23

40 41 42

6

22

43

44 45 46

7

20

47

9

3 19

70

51

55

10

18

69

54

49

56

17

68

53

50

57

16

52

58

11

PEDESTAL
PANEL
ASSEMBLY

59

12

67

13

66

60

15

65

LEFT CONSOLE

14

63

64

RIGHT CONSOLE

14

The rear cockpit of the two-seat TAV-8B, in which it can
be seen that many of the instruments of the Harrier II are
the same as those of the F-18. In the upper part of the
instrument panel the HUD can be seen, under the UFC (Up
Front Control) and a set of clock type instruments which
can be used in the case of failure of the digital systems.
On the left part the DDI (Digital Display Indicator) can be
seen, along with the ODU (Option Display Unit) above the
Armament Control Panel underneath. To the left of the DDI
the Armament Master Switch and the switch for launching
the firing of infrared flares can be seen and to the right
there are parameter indicators for the engine and the
amount of fuel in the tanks. The stick is also very similar
to that of the F-18. On the seat there is ring with yellow
and black bands for ejection and a green ring to activate
the emergency oxygen. In the glass dome of the cockpit
there are two small lamps on each strip, one to illuminate
the instrument panel and the other to illuminate the pilot's
kneeboard. (Luis Díaz-Bedia Astor)

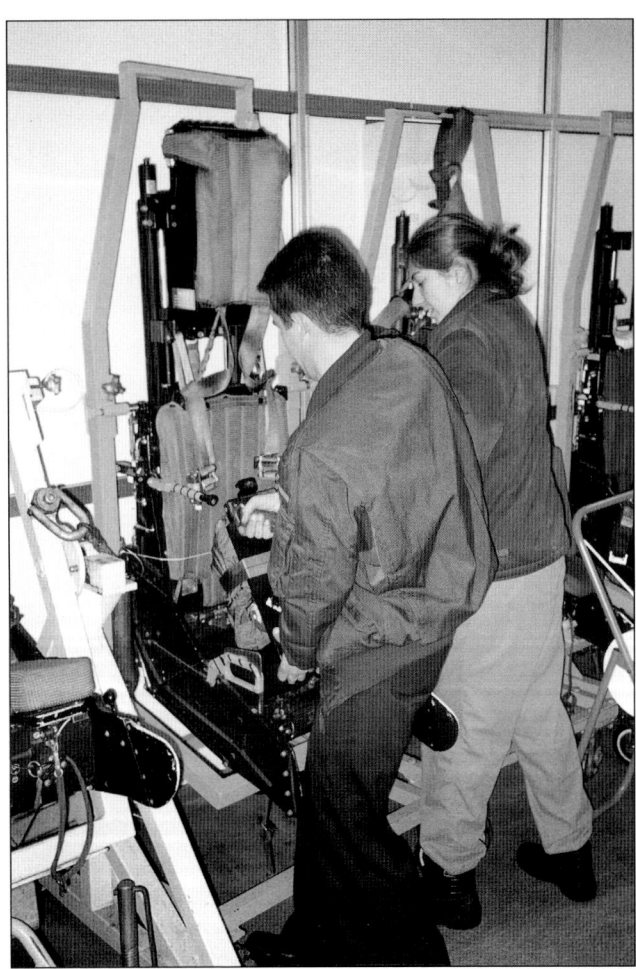

An officer and a sailor of the Ninth Squadron carrying out a check of an ejector seat. *(Luis Díaz-Bedia Astor)*

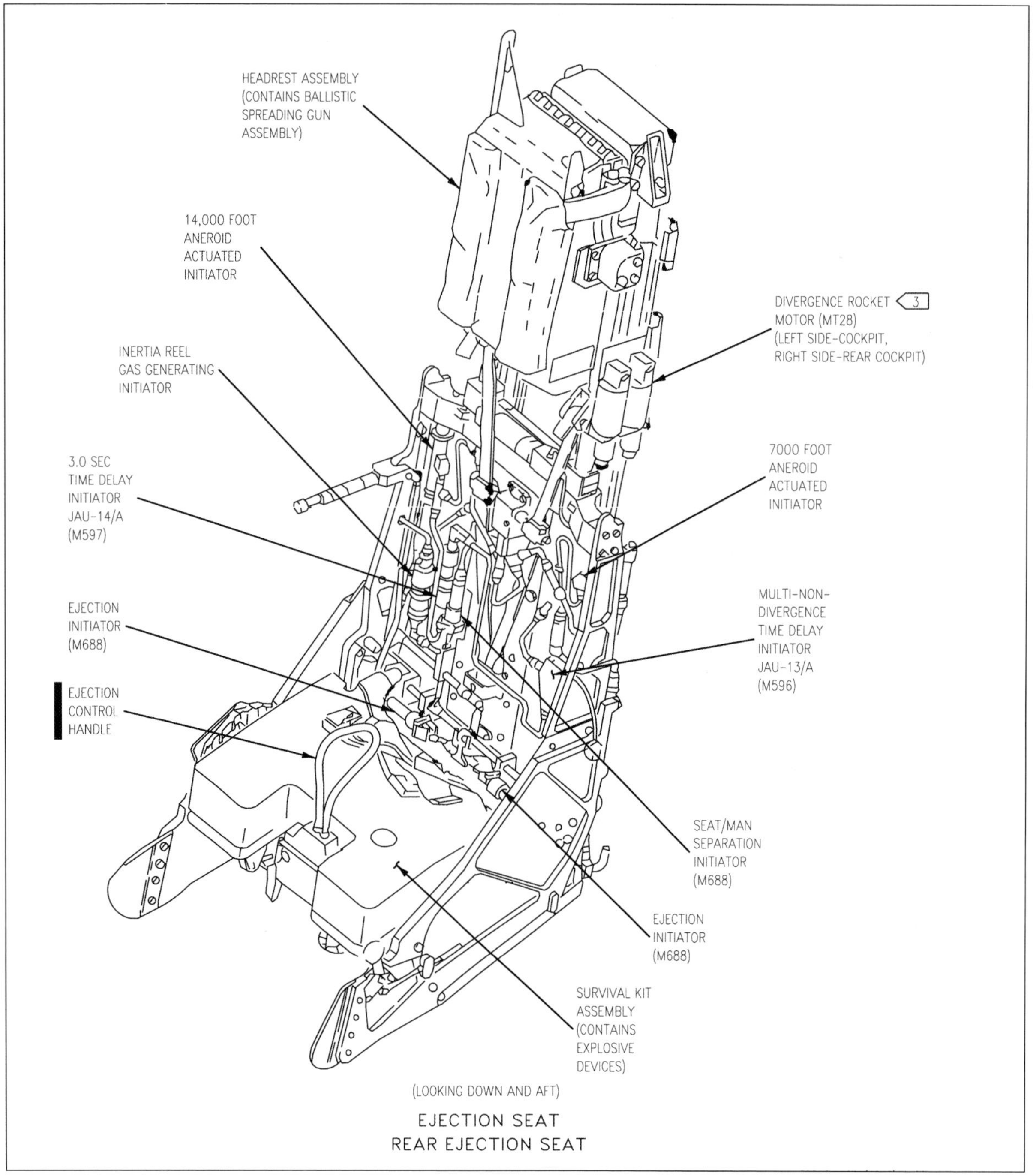

HEADREST ASSEMBLY
(CONTAINS BALLISTIC
SPREADING GUN
ASSEMBLY)

14,000 FOOT
ANEROID
ACTUATED
INITIATOR

DIVERGENCE ROCKET 〈 3
MOTOR (MT28)
(LEFT SIDE-COCKPIT,
RIGHT SIDE-REAR COCKPIT)

INERTIA REEL
GAS GENERATING
INITIATOR

7000 FOOT
ANEROID
ACTUATED
INITIATOR

3.0 SEC
TIME DELAY
INITIATOR
JAU-14/A
(M597)

MULTI-NON-
DIVERGENCE
TIME DELAY
INITIATOR
JAU-13/A
(M596)

EJECTION
INITIATOR
(M688)

EJECTION
CONTROL
HANDLE

SEAT/MAN
SEPARATION
INITIATOR
(M688)

EJECTION
INITIATOR
(M688)

SURVIVAL KIT
ASSEMBLY
(CONTAINS
EXPLOSIVE
DEVICES)

(LOOKING DOWN AND AFT)

EJECTION SEAT
REAR EJECTION SEAT

The Pegasus F-402-RR-408 engine before being fitted in an AV-8B Plus, in the hangar of the Ninth Squadron of the Air force. *(Luis Díaz-Bedia Astor)*

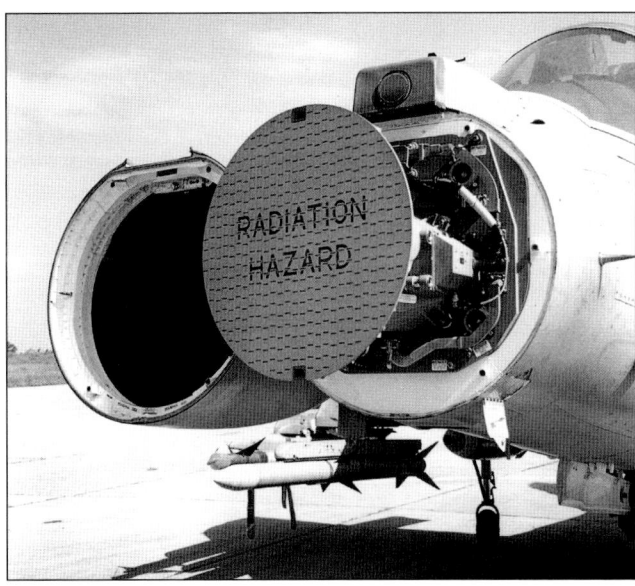

The APG-65 radar aerial, which has had to be made smaller than that of the F-18 to fit inside the nose of the AV-8B Plus. *(Luis Díaz-Bedia Astor)*

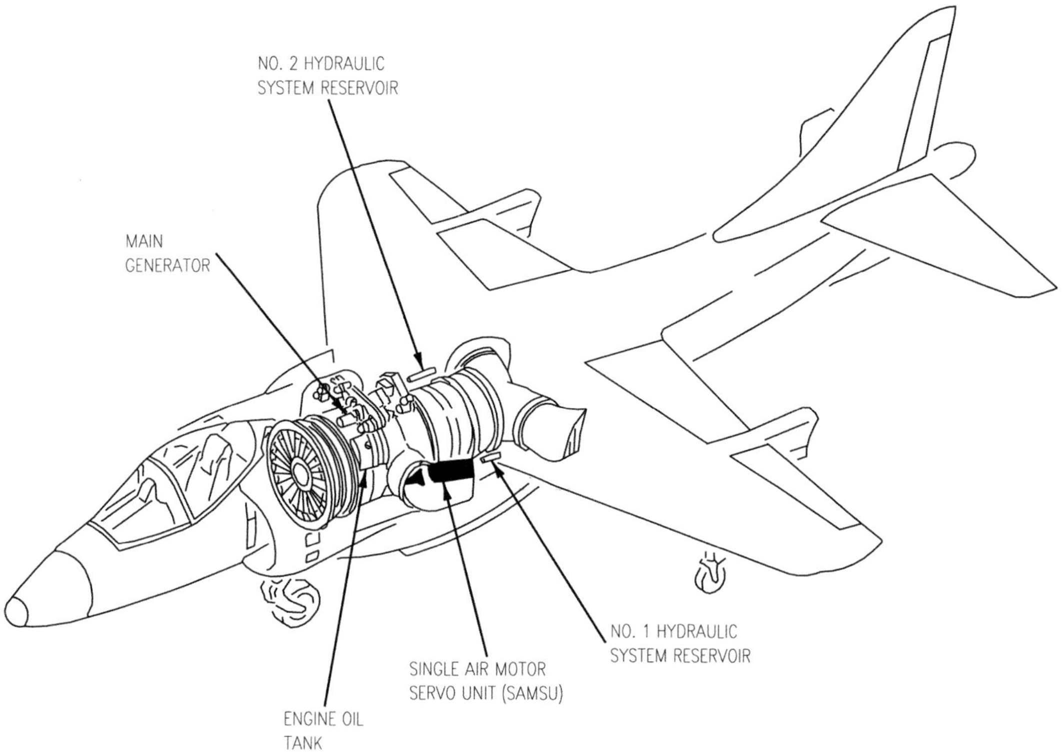

NO. 2 HYDRAULIC SYSTEM RESERVOIR

MAIN GENERATOR

NO. 1 HYDRAULIC SYSTEM RESERVOIR

SINGLE AIR MOTOR SERVO UNIT (SAMSU)

ENGINE OIL TANK

FLAMMABLE LIQUIDS		
COMPONENT	FLUID/OIL	
ENGINE OIL TANK, MAIN GENERATOR, SINGLE AIR MOTOR SERVO UNIT (SAMSU)	OIL MIL-L-23699	ENGINE, 11:00 ENGINE, 12:00 DOOR 29
NO. 1 AND NO. 2 HYDRAULIC SYSTEM RESERVOIR	HYDRAULIC FLUID MIL-H-83282	FS 345.00 LBL 27.00 WL 96.00 (NO. 1)
		FS 345.00 RBL 27.00 WL 96.00 (NO. 2)

A Cobra follows the directions of a flight deck director to arrive at a launching spot from which he has to begin operations for take-off. *(Luis Díaz-Bedia Astor)*

An AV-8B aircraft on the Ski-jump of the Príncipe de Asturias, docked at the Brest arsenal in April 2000, at the beginning of the *LINKED SEAS 2000* exercise. The protection given by the aircraft's enormous air inlets which helps to avoid FOD (Foreign Object Damage) in the turbines can be seen. The firing system lens, as well as the pitot tubes and attack angle indicator are also hidden underneath the protective hoods. Under the nose are the front *puffer* of the Reaction Control System and a set of small aerials in a small cone belonging to the radar alert. In the nose gear the approach light can be clearly seen. The deck clamps can be clearly seen in the nose gear, main gear and outriggers. *(Luis Díaz-Bedia Astor)*

An AV-8B aircraft in the elevator on the stern of the *Príncipe de Asturias* aircraft carrier during the *LINKED SEAS 2000* exercise. Hanging from the left side is an external fuel tank, with a capacity of approximately 2,000 lbs. The Harrier II can carry two or four of these tanks, giving it a considerable amount of autonomy, the internal tanks hold a total of 7,500 lbs – although at the expense of a reduction in the arms that it can carry. *(Luis Díaz-Bedia Astor)*

An AV-8B Plus returning to Rota after a training flight, on the outskirts of Chipiona. *(Luis Díaz-Bedia Astor)*

► View of the nose section of the two-seat TAV-8B of the Ninth Squadron. The cockpits open laterally instead of longitudinally as in the case of the AV-8B. The two weathervanes used by the pilots to gauge the wind when undertaking VSTOL landings and take-offs can be seen. *(Luis Díaz-Bedia Astor)*

▼ The 01-922 two-seater in the parking space of the Rota naval base, on November 26, 2003, preparing for a flight. The empennage is larger than that of a single-seater aircraft, in order to compensate for the aerodynamic effect produced by the increase in the nose section and the length of the aircraft when a second cockpit is added. *(Luis Díaz-Bedia Astor)*

◄ An AV-8B Plus flying over the Atlantic near to the *Príncipe de Asturias*, during the *LINKED SEAS* exercise in May 2000. *(Luis Díaz-Bedia Astor)*

▼ An AV-8B aircraft in the parking area of the Zaragoza air base during the firing detachment of the Ninth Squadron in March 2000. The second is a Plus, which can be clearly distinguished by the two side chaff and flares dispensers situated on the upper part of the fuselage behind the wing. *(Luis Díaz-Bedia Astor)*

MORE SCHIFFER TITLES

www.schifferbooks.com

Boeing B-52: A Documentary History Walter J. Boyne. Conceived in 1948, first flown in 1952 and projected still to be in front-line service in the 21st century, the Boeing B-52 Stratofortress is one of the most extraordinary aircraft in history. Features a comprehensive history of the development of the U.S. heavy bomber, and the enormous number of modifications and changes which have kept the aircraft viable.
Size: 8.5"x11" • 200 bw photos • 160pp.
ISBN: 0-88740-600-9 • hard • $29.95

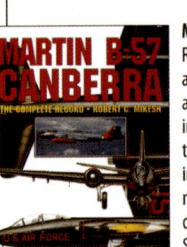

Martin B-57 Canberra: The Complete Record Robert C. Mikesh. No story about one type of aircraft could be more complete than this coverage about the B-57. A brief history of its British inception sets the stage for the conversion that took place to American standards for production in the U.S. The Canberra was needed to fill the night intruder role in the USAF that was identified during the Korean War and later Vietnam.
Size: 8.5"x11" • 420 color/bw photos • 208pp.
ISBN: 0-88740-661-0 • hard • $45.00

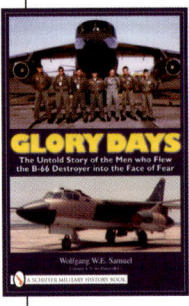

Glory Days: The Untold Story of the Men who Flew the B-66 Destroyer into the Face of Fear Wolfgang W.E. Samuel. The untold story of an airplane and its brave flyers who valiantly served our nation in time of war. The two EB-66 equipped combat squadrons flying from bases in Thailand against North Vietnam earned the Presidential Unit Citation for valor in combat, numerous Outstanding Unit Awards with V-device, and equivalent U.S. Navy citations.
Size: 6"x9" • over 80 bw images • 464 pp.
ISBN: 978-0-7643-3086-5 • hard • $35.00

Convair B-58 Hustler Bill Holder. The legendary B-58, one of the most interesting bombers to reach operational status, and had an appearance – even though designed in the 1940s – that would not look out of date in the 21st century. The first USAF delta-wing bomber was the Mach 2 Hustler that had the performance of a fighter.
Size: 8.5"x11" • 180 color/bw photos • 64pp.
ISBN: 978-0-7643-1468-1 • soft • $19.99

Northrop Grumman B-2 Spirit: An Illustrated History Bill Holder. It has been called the most amazing and unbelievable aircraft of the 20th century. One look at the bat-like lines of the USAF's stealthy Spirit bomber quickly confirms this. But that futuristic shape has lineage back to the 1940s when the Northrop Company designed and built the B-35 and B-49.
Size: 8.5"x11" • 150 color/bw photos • 80pp.
ISBN: 0-7643-0591-3 • soft • $19.95

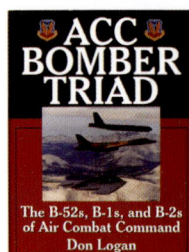

ACC Bomber Triad: The B-52s, B-1s, and B-2s of Air Combat Command Don Logan. This book presents a roll call of ACC's bombers with photos and history of all 208 bombers since joining ACC in June 1992. Also included are all of the bombers' weapons. Includes eighty unit and special purpose flight suit patches.
Size: 8.5"x11" • 780 color photos • 304pp.
ISBN: 0-7643-0680-4 • hard • $59.95

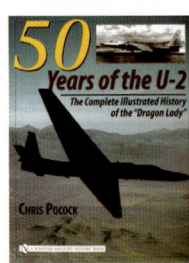

50 Years of the U-2: The Complete Illustrated History of Lockheed's Legendary "Dragon Lady" Chris Pocock. The long story of the Dragon Lady is amazing, and complex; this book tells it all, in unprecedented detail, from the early days overflying the Soviet Union under CIA sponsorship, to the Cuban Missile Crisis, and on to the Vietnam War, epic missions over Communist China, and its key role in Desert Storm, over Bosnia and Kosovo, Afghanistan and Iraq.
Size: 8.5"x11" • 450 color/bw photos • 440pp.
ISBN: 978-0-7643-2346-1 • hard • $69.99

The U-2 Spyplane - Toward the Unknown: A New History of the Early Years Chris Pocock. The full story of the development and early use of the U-2 has never been properly told – until now. This book describes in vivid detail how the high-flying spyplane was conceived, designed, built, and deployed in record time.
Size: 6"x9" • 110 bw/color images • 288pp.
ISBN: 978-0-7643-1113-0 • hard • $35.00

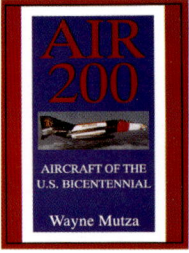

Air 200: Aircraft of the U.S. Bicentennial Wayne Mutza. Though Bicentennial aircraft schemes and markings, along with many of the aircraft of that period, have all but faded into obscurity, this colorful volume not only preserves their images, but reflects the spirit that prevailed during that historic period in U.S. aviation history.
Size: 8.5"x11" • 190 color/bw photos • 104pp.
ISBN: 0-7643-0388-0 • soft • $19.95

One-of-a-Kind Research Aircraft: A History of In-Flight Simulators, Testbeds, & Prototypes Markman & Holder. Covered in this unique volume are the great variety of Inflight Simulation Aircraft, Testbed Aircraft, and Prototype Aircraft.
Size: 8.5"x11" • over 200 photos • 152pp.
ISBN: 0-88740-797-8 • hard • $45.00

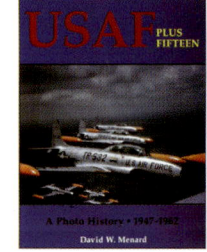

USAF Plus Fifteen: A Photo History 1947-62 David W. Menard. Full color photo history of the early USAF covers the great variety of fighters, bombers, transport, helicopters and many other aircraft in use during this period.
Size: 8.5"x11" • over 400 color photos • 144pp.
ISBN: 0-88740-483-9 • soft • $24.95

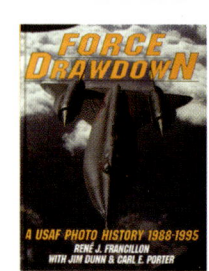

Force Drawdown: A USAF Photo History 1988-95 Francillon/Dunn/Porter. The end of the Cold War created a golden opportunity for reducing the defense burden and providing taxpayers with a "Peace Dividend." This book provides a rich pictorial record of aircraft (including old and new markings) and units which no longer exist, and offers a visual chronicle of organizational changes between 1988-1995.
Size: 8.5"x11" • over 410 color photos • 144pp.
ISBN: 0-88740-777-3 • hard • $29.95